STEP-UP Books

are written especially for children who have outgrown begin-
ning readers. In this exciting series:

- the words are harder (but not too hard)
- there's more text (but it's still in big print)
- there are plenty of illustrations (but the books aren't picture
  books)
- the subject matter has been carefully chosen to appeal to
  young readers who want to find out about the world around
  them. They'll love these informative and lively books.

ANIMALS BUILD AMAZING HOMES

- One home is as narrow as a pin.
- Another weighs a ton.
- Still another is made of air bubbles!

Here are the stories of 15 different animal homes—and the animals who build them. Each house is exactly right for the life
its owner leads. And each one is amazing!

Animals Build

by Hedda Nussbaum

Amazing Homes

illustrated by Christopher Santoro

Step-Up Books ⌐ ⌐ Random House
New York

For my mother and father

The author and publisher wish to thank Barbara Neill, Senior Instructor, Alexander M. White Natural Science Center, American Museum of Natural History, for help in the preparation of this book.

Thanks are also due to Dr. Kraig Adler, Division of Biological Sciences, Cornell University; Dr. Klaus Busse, Zoologisches Forschungsinstitut und Museum Alexander Koenig, Bonn; Neil Cleminson, British Broadcasting Corporation; Dr. Charles J. Cole, Herpatology Department, American Museum of Natural History; Alice Gray, Entomology Department, American Museum of Natural History; Joseph Herring, Louisiana Wildlife and Fisheries Commission; William Jorgensen; Raymond L. Linder, South Dakota Cooperative Wildlife Research Unit, South Dakota State University; and Dr. Edward O. Wilson, Museum of Comparative Zoology, Harvard University.

Library of Congress Cataloging in Publication Data
Nussbaum, Hedda. Animals build amazing homes. (Step-up books; 29) SUMMARY: Describes the construction and the function of the homes built by 15 different animals. 1. Animals, Habitations of—Juvenile literature. [I. Animals—Habitations] I. Santoro, Christopher. II. Title
QL756.N87 591.5´6 79-11326 ISBN: 0-394-83850-5 ISBN: 0-394-93850-X (lib. bdg.)

Manufactured in the United States of America   1 2 3 4 5 6 7 8 9 0

Contents

All Kinds of Homes

A house built from leaves . . . a castle with
no light inside . . . a home made of
air bubbles . . . a house with its door
underwater. . . . What are these strange
homes? They are all houses built by animals.

All over the world, animals build or find
amazing homes. And no one ever tells them
how. Most animals are born knowing how to
make a home. A few learn by watching their
parents.

No two kinds of animals have exactly the same kind of house. And not all use their houses for the same thing. Each house suits the needs of its owner.

Many homes are good places to hide from enemies. Others are good for storing food. Many animals use their houses just for laying eggs and raising babies. Others live in theirs all the time. Some just sleep in the house.

The stories in this book tell about some animal homes. They are all different. And they are all amazing!

Home Is a Castle

Picture 50,000 busy insects. They are all blind. Each one is less than an inch long. They are building a house. Someday it will be 18 feet tall!

The insects are African mound-building termites. They make their homes from sand, soil, and saliva (spit). They build up the walls tiny bit by tiny bit. Many years go by before a mound gets large.

The homes of African mound builders look like castles. At the center of a castle live the king and queen. The queen is much larger than the other termites. She is more than four inches long and very fat. She looks like a white sausage. She is full of eggs. Each day she lays thousands!

Some of the eggs become soldiers. They protect the castle. Others become workers. They feed wood, plants, and saliva to the king and queen. They build up the mound.

Workers also take care of the indoor gardens. African mound builders grow their own fungus (FUN-gus) plants. Fungus is one of the things they eat.

A termite castle has many rooms. It has special rooms for the fungus gardens. It has rooms where eggs are stored. It also has rooms for young termites.

The castle is very dark inside. It has no windows or doors. But the termites don't mind. They need no light because they are blind. The castle never gets stuffy. Fresh air gets in through the castle walls. The termites themselves go in and out through a few underground tunnels.

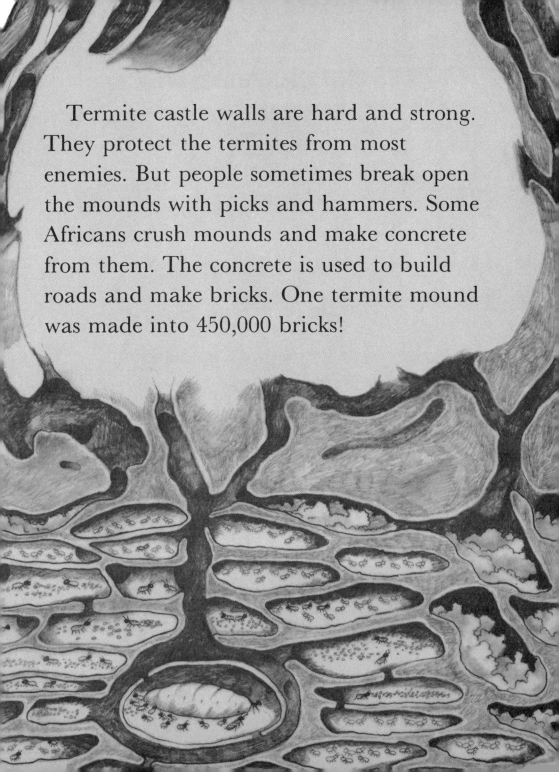

Termite castle walls are hard and strong. They protect the termites from most enemies. But people sometimes break open the mounds with picks and hammers. Some Africans crush mounds and make concrete from them. The concrete is used to build roads and make bricks. One termite mound was made into 450,000 bricks!

The Old Swimming Hole

What animal is big, black, scaly, and has its own swimming hole? Give up? The answer is the American alligator.

Alligators like to live in water that is a few feet deep. But alligators that live in marshes have a problem. Marsh water is deep only when there is a lot of rain. In dry times, the water gets very low. So the alligator digs its own pond.

These ponds are called gator holes. They can be as large as 25 feet wide and 10 feet deep. Gator holes reach water that lies a short way under the ground. They never dry up.

An alligator makes its pond by digging out the marsh mud. It pushes the mud with its snout and the sides of its body. The mud piles up around the hole. It forms an underwater wall. Plants grow on it. They stick out of the water. They mark the edges of the alligator's pond.

Fish, frogs, and other animals share the swimming hole. But a hungry alligator will eat any small animal it sees. So some animals in the gator hole become the alligator's lunch!

A gator hole is home to an alligator. In winter it doesn't leave home at all. The alligator feels slow and lazy. So it stays in the water and rests. On very cold days it crawls inside a tunnel that it has dug. The tunnel is in the side of the pond. There the alligator keeps warm.

Alligators stay in their ponds until spring. Then they start feeling lively again. They visit dry land. The males and females meet there and mate.

Soon after mating, each female builds a land nest of grass, leaves, and mud. In it she lays about 35 eggs. She covers up the nest and begins to keep watch for enemies. If any come near the nest, she chases them away. She watches the nest from her swimming hole. But from time to time she comes out for a closer look.

After about two months, the babies hatch
inside the nest. They begin to call out,
"Rumpf, rumpf!" That seems to mean, "Let
me out!" And the mother does just that. She
opens the nest, and out come the tiny
alligators. Where do they go? Right into the
water! Usually the nearest water is their
mother's gator hole.

What a sight—mother alligator and her
35 babies in their private swimming hole!

The Trap

All spiders make webs. Right? Wrong! A few kinds of spiders don't. These are the trap-door spiders. They live in southern and western parts of the United States.

Most spiders catch their food in their webs. But a trap-door spider must catch its food in another way. It uses the amazing trap door of its house to help it.

This spider's home is a narrow hole in the ground. It is called a burrow. The spider digs the burrow with two of its eight legs. It also uses its two fangs. These are sharp points that hang down from the spider's jaws. After the hole is dug, the spider lines it with silk. The silk is made in the spider's body.

Next comes the famous
trap door. The spider
builds it from layers of
silk and earth. The door
fits the opening of the
burrow perfectly. A silk
hinge at one side holds
the door in place. The
trap door can open
and close easily. The
spider puts earth
and pieces of plants
on top of the door.
When closed, it
looks like the
ground around it.

Now the house is finished. The spider
waits inside until dark. Then it holds the
trap door open a tiny bit. Soon an insect
walks too near. The spider jumps. Up flies
the trap door! The spider pulls the insect
into the burrow. The trap door falls closed.
Dinner at last!

If an enemy wants the spider for ITS dinner, the trap door helps keep the spider safe. The door has some little holes on the inside. The spider puts its fangs in two of the holes and pulls hard. At the same time, it pushes its four back legs against the wall of the burrow. The door is held shut. Only a very strong enemy can pull it open.

The trap door keeps out more than enemies. It keeps out rain and snow, too. It also helps keep the burrow cool in summer and warm in winter.

A female trap-door spider lays her eggs at the bottom of her burrow. After the little spiders hatch, they stay in the burrow at least a year. Then they dig their own houses. Each burrow has its own little trap door. And inside each one, a spider is waiting to . . . SNAP!

Treetop Apartments

Did you ever see a bird's nest that looks like a giant haystack? Probably not, unless you have been to the dry parts of southern Africa. That's where the social weaverbirds live. They build huge straw houses.

Most birds make one nest for one family. But not the social weavers. Groups of them work together to build an apartment house in a tree. One family lives in each apartment. Often more than 100 families live in each house. A house sometimes weighs more than 2,000 pounds (900 kilograms).

The house is made of dry grasses and small twigs. Some kinds of weaverbirds really weave grasses into small nests. But the social weavers don't weave. They just stick grasses and twigs into a big pile. The sides of the pile are smooth. And they slant downward. When rains come, the water runs off the nest.

Inside the house, each male and female pair make their own apartment. It is a round room with a hallway to the outside. The birds make it by biting off twigs from the underside of the house. They line the apartment with soft grass. The birds stick short, sharp straws around the doorway. These help keep out tree snakes.

As the years pass, social weaverbirds add to their apartment house. All the birds do some work, even young birds. They add more grasses to the sides of the nest. The house gets taller and wider. It holds more and more apartments.

A nest may grow for 100 years. Finally it gets too heavy for the branch it is on. Then . . . CRACK . . . the branch breaks. And down falls the nest, birds and all! Everyone gets out fast. Good-bye, birds! The time has come to build some new apartment houses.

Wax Wonders

Bees are famous for making honey. But honeybees make something else, too—wax! People use beeswax in candles and chewing gum. Bees use it to make their homes.

Honeybees build tiny wax rooms called cells. The cells are always the same sizes and shapes. People would need rulers and other tools to build such perfect cells. But the bees do it all by themselves.

The cells are the inside part of the bees' home. The home is called a hive. Bees set up their hive in a hollow place. Some bees pick a hollow log or a hollow tree. Others find a man-made box.

Inside every hive lives a queen bee. She lays hundreds of eggs every day. The hive also has worker bees. They are all females. One of their jobs is building the amazing wax cells.

To start making cells, a group of workers gather together. They hang from the top of the hive. They grab on to each other's legs. They form chains. Side by side, the chains make a wall of bees.

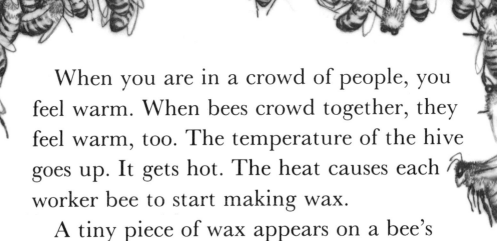

When you are in a crowd of people, you feel warm. When bees crowd together, they feel warm, too. The temperature of the hive goes up. It gets hot. The heat causes each worker bee to start making wax.

A tiny piece of wax appears on a bee's belly. The bee puts it in her mouth and chews it like gum. It becomes soft. With her tongue, the worker smears the wax on the hive's ceiling. Other bees add more bits of wax to this one. Bit by bit, together they build a cell. No bee ever builds a whole cell by herself.

A small piece of the two cell walls looks like this. →

The bees keep building down from the ceiling. When they are finished, they have two walls of perfect cells. Each cell has six sides. The walls fit together back to back. Up to 1,000 bees helped make the cells. No one gave them orders. But somehow the job came out right.

The queen bee keeps laying eggs. The workers keep making more double walls of cells. Some of the cells hold food—honey, and pollen from flowers. Other cells hold eggs and young bees.

After a while the hive becomes too small for all the bees in it. Then the workers build special large round cells. Queen bees are raised in them. Before the first new queen comes out, the old queen leaves. She takes half the bees in the hive with her. Off they fly to build a new wax wonder.

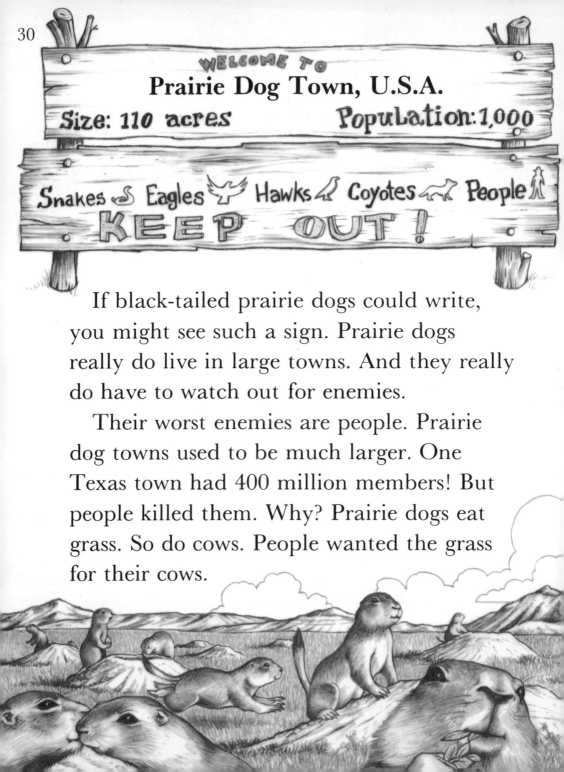

WELCOME TO
Prairie Dog Town, U.S.A.
Size: 110 acres   Population: 1,000

Snakes ∽ Eagles ✲ Hawks ⟅ Coyotes ⟅ People ⚡
KEEP OUT!

If black-tailed prairie dogs could write, you might see such a sign. Prairie dogs really do live in large towns. And they really do have to watch out for enemies.

Their worst enemies are people. Prairie dog towns used to be much larger. One Texas town had 400 million members! But people killed them. Why? Prairie dogs eat grass. So do cows. People wanted the grass for their cows.

Prairie dogs are not dogs at all. They are a kind of ground squirrel. Or you might say underground squirrel—because prairie dogs live underground.

On top of their homes only little mounds of earth show. In the middle of each mound, a hole leads underground. The mound slants away from the hole. So when it rains, water on the ground does not run into the house. A mound is a good place to stand. From the top of it a prairie dog can see a faraway enemy.

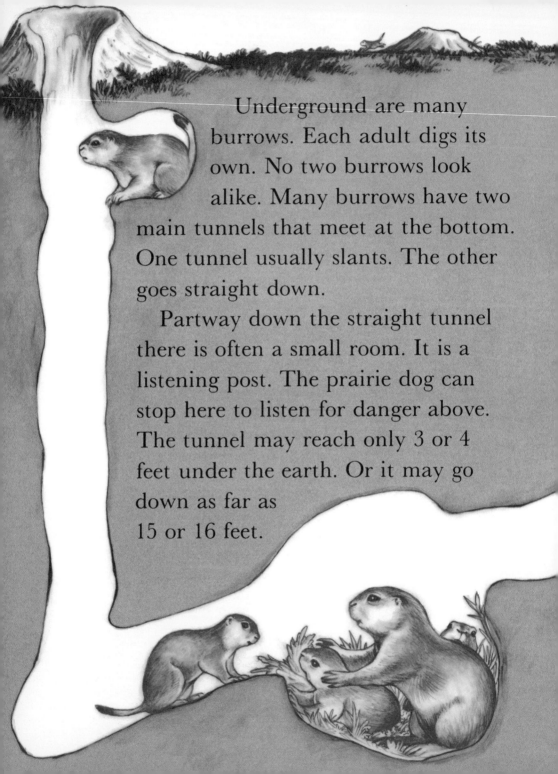

Underground are many burrows. Each adult digs its own. No two burrows look alike. Many burrows have two main tunnels that meet at the bottom. One tunnel usually slants. The other goes straight down.

Partway down the straight tunnel there is often a small room. It is a listening post. The prairie dog can stop here to listen for danger above. The tunnel may reach only 3 or 4 feet under the earth. Or it may go down as far as 15 or 16 feet.

The slanted tunnel has rooms along it. There are one or more sleeping rooms with grass nests inside. A storeroom holds food for winter. Sometimes there is even a toilet room.

The prairie dogs in each town belong to groups called clans. Most clans are made up of one male, a few females, and their children. The prairie dogs in a clan are great friends. But they attack any adult from another clan who comes near.

Only the children are welcomed by everyone. They can visit the whole town. Everyone plays with them. Any female will feed them. But one day they get too big. Then they are chased back to their own clan.

When danger is near, the whole town works together. If a prairie dog sees a hawk, it barks. The bark is a warning to everyone. Prairie dogs all over town jump into their burrows. Many stop at the listening post.

When all is quiet, some prairie dogs peek out the top. If the hawk is gone, someone gives an all-clear bark. Then the prairie dogs come out again.

The Mystery Nest

Look at the picture on this page. What do you think it shows? Did you guess a bird's nest? It surely looks like one. But it isn't. It is the nest of a very different kind of animal. Which one? That is the mystery. Turn the page to find the answer.

The picture shows the nest of the tiny European harvest mouse. Inside the nest are five baby mice. Each one is less than an inch long. You can see their mother outside the nest on this page. She is its builder.

Before her babies are born, a mother harvest mouse goes to work. With her teeth she cuts tall grasses or grain stalks into strips. She weaves them into a hollow ball. Then she climbs into the nest. She lines the inside with small pieces of plants.

Here is another mystery. How does she get in? Where is the door? There is none! She pushes her way through the grasses. Then the hole she makes disappears. The grasses spring back into place.

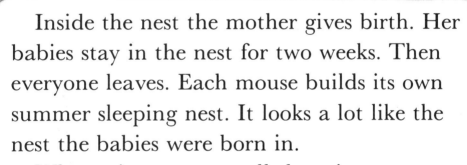

Inside the nest the mother gives birth. Her babies stay in the nest for two weeks. Then everyone leaves. Each mouse builds its own summer sleeping nest. It looks a lot like the nest the babies were born in.

When winter comes, all the mice move. They keep warm in a barn or a hole in the ground.

What happens when the weather gets warm? That is no mystery. The harvest mice return to the tall grasses once again.

A Fussy Shopper

A hermit crab is a funny-looking animal. It runs around with another animal's shell on its back!

Many sea animals grow their own shells. The shells are like houses for them. Their bodies are soft. The shells are hard. They protect the animals from enemies.

The hermit crab has no shell house of its own. So it borrows one. In fact, it borrows more than one. As the hermit crab grows, it gets too big for its house. So from time to time, it must find a new one.

Hermit crabs are very picky about their houses. Some like pretty shells with bright colors. Some like shells with seaweed stuck to them. But every crab must have a shell that fits just right. And the shell must be shaped like a snail's shell.

Most of the time a hermit crab finds an empty shell from a dead animal. But once in a while it attacks a live animal inside the shell. Then it gets dinner and a house at the same time!

In hot countries there are hermit crabs that live on beaches. But in other places hermit crabs live in the ocean. They are found in quiet, shallow water. You can often see one go house hunting along a bay beach or mud flat. The sight will make you laugh. The crab acts just like a fussy shopper!

The crab runs along the sand under the water. It stops at every likely shell. It touches the shell with its long feelers. It picks up the shell with its claws and turns the shell around. It sticks a claw inside.

If the crab does not like the shell, it goes on to the next one. If the shell seems right, the crab puts it on. Quickly the animal jumps out of its old shell. Quickly it slips into the new one, back end first. If you blink, you might miss the switch.

Most of the crab is in the shell. But its head, claws, and many of its legs stick out.

Will the crab keep its new shell house? Maybe. The crab makes some tests. Does the shell leave room to grow? Yet is it snug enough to stay on? Can the crab's claws cover the whole opening? They must. When danger is near, the crab will pull itself all the way into the shell. It will cover the opening with its claws.

Suppose the shell doesn't fit just right. Then the crab runs off again to find a new house. What a fussy fellow!

The Strangest Nest

Many animals make nests for their eggs and babies. But the Darwin frog of Chile does not MAKE a nest for its young. The male has one built into his body!

In the spring, male Darwin frogs look for mates. A few males sit together. They make croaking noises to bring females to them. When they croak, their vocal pouches swell up. A vocal pouch is a soft area of skin around a male frog's throat. It blows up like a balloon. That makes the croaking louder.

Male Darwin frogs have big vocal pouches but small voices. They sound like baby ducks peeping!

A few females hear the sound. They come hopping over to the males. Each one lays about 35 eggs on damp earth. The eggs have thin skins instead of hard shells. On top of the eggs, the males lay a thick liquid from their bodies. Now the eggs are fertilized (FUR-tuh-lized). They can grow into tadpoles—baby frogs.

The females leave. The males stay and watch over all the eggs. They make sure no hungry animals eat the eggs.

Two or three weeks pass. The eggs are almost ready to hatch. Tiny tadpoles show through them.

Now the father frogs do something strange. Each one picks up some eggs with his tongue. Does he eat the eggs? No. He slides them into his vocal pouch! It has plenty of room for eggs. The male Darwin frog has a VERY large pouch. It covers his whole neck, chest, and belly.

The tadpoles soon come out of their eggs. They don't look at all like frogs. They have long tails and no legs. The tadpoles stay inside the vocal pouch for 12 weeks. They live on food that is stored in their bodies.

What about the father? Can he swallow food without swallowing the babies? Yes. He has no trouble eating. But he does not croak while the tadpoles are inside.

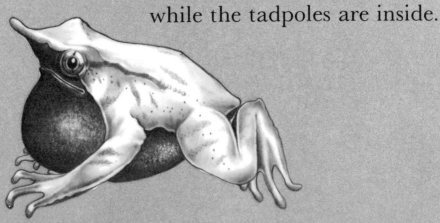

During the 12 weeks the tadpoles change. Slowly they grow legs and feet. They lose their tails. At last they look like frogs. Each one is about one-half inch long.

The father is not much more than one inch long himself. His pouch bulges with young frogs. He looks as if he might explode! It is time for the babies to leave. So the father moves his pouch in and out quickly. He pushes out the little frogs. Out they go, the same way they came in—through their father's mouth.

How to Sink a Ship

Can an inch-long shipworm sink a ship? Yes! Well, almost. One shipworm cannot sink a ship by itself. But together many shipworms can.

A shipworm is not a worm at all. It is a sea animal with a shell. But it looks like a worm. Its shell is at one end of a long wormy body. It lives in oceans around the world.

Shipworms make their homes in wet wood. Once all ships were wooden. These animals often got inside. That is how shipworms got their name. Today fewer ships and boats are made of wood. Most wooden boats are soaked in oil. Shipworms don't like the oil. So they go away and find some other wood. Any sailor who forgets to oil his boat is in trouble!

A shipworm starts its home when it is one or two weeks old. It uses its rough shell to drill into the wet wood. The baby shipworm is as thin as a pin. So its hole is only as big as a pinhole. No one would notice it.

Once the shipworm is inside the wood, it grows. It keeps drilling. The hole inside gets longer and wider. The animal lines the hole with the same hard stuff that its shell is made of.

Hundreds of shipworms can live in one small piece of wood. They may grow six inches long—or even more. The wood becomes full of deep holes. From outside, the holes still look like tiny pinholes. But inside the wood is no longer strong. In storms many ships used to fall apart. And they would sink! All because of the little shipworm.

The Secret House

In a pond is a secret underwater house. Its roof looks like a little island sticking out of the water. There is no door. Only underwater tunnels lead to the house. It is safe from all enemies.

Who lives here? A gang of robbers? Spies? Pirates? No! A family of beavers!

The beavers' home is called a lodge. The lodge is built in water at least four feet deep. Sometimes beavers build their lodge in a deep river. But often they can find only a shallow stream. So they make part of the stream deeper.

Beavers make water deep by building a dam. They pile mud, sticks, and stones across the stream. This dam slows down the flow of water. Water gets higher and deeper in front of the dam. The deep water forms a pond.

In the pond the beavers build their lodge.
They work at night when enemies can't see
them. First they pile up mud and stones for
a base. Then the beavers cut down thin,
young trees with their teeth. They cut up
the trees into sticks and carry them to the
pond. With the sticks in their mouths, they
swim to the base. On it the beavers pile the
sticks into a big mound. Most of this mound
is under the water. Only the top pokes
up above.

Next the beavers dive underwater. They make tunnels by digging up into the mound. They use their teeth and front paws. Deep inside the mound the beavers dig out a room. The room is big enough for two parents and four children to sleep in. It is above the water line, so it stays nice and dry.

Next the beavers add mud to the lodge. They poke the mud in between the sticks. Now rain and cold air can't get inside. Together, the mud and sticks make the lodge very strong. Your parents could walk on it. The lodge would not break. No hungry animal can break in.

At the top of the lodge is a small area without mud. Air can get in and out through it. So the beavers have fresh air in their house.

In the water near the lodge, beavers pile up whole small trees. The bark and leaves are their food for the winter. The beavers save the branches for fixing their dam. Or they may use them to make the lodge bigger.

The beavers stay inside the lodge all winter. It is warm, dry, and safe. Not even pirates could have a better hiding place!

Good Enough to Eat

Would you eat a bird's nest? Some people do. The Chinese make soup from the nests of certain swiftlets. The nests are made of pure saliva!

The swiftlets that make these nests are sometimes called sea swallows. The birds live in parts of southeast Asia. They build their nests in dark caves. Many hundreds of swiftlets share a cave.

A male and a female build the nest together. They usually work at night.

First they pick a spot on the cave wall. Then they outline the shape of the nest with their tongues. They make a curved line of saliva on the wall. Swiftlets' saliva is very thick. It hardens soon after it hits the air.

The birds keep placing more saliva over the outline. They build out and away from the wall.

The finished nest is shaped like half of a bowl. It is white. It looks and feels like dried glue.

Swiftlets' nests are often in caves that are hard to reach. Many of the caves are next to the sea. Some cave doors are underwater. People can enter them only when the water is low. Other caves can be entered only through very narrow tunnels.

Long ago, the Chinese trained monkeys to gather the swiftlets' nests. Today people do the job. They bring lamps and ladders to the dark caves. Then they climb the ladders and take the nests off the walls.

Cooks who make bird's nest soup
usually don't see a whole nest. Some cooks
buy little balls made from ground-up
nests. Other cooks use broken pieces of nest.
They soak the balls or pieces in water to
make them soft. Then they cook them in
water with some ham and chicken.

What do the nests taste like? They have
little taste of their own. The nests pick up
flavors from the other foods in the soup.
They make the other flavors stronger. But
why not find out for yourself? The next time
you go to a Chinese restaurant, ask for bird's
nest soup. You may love it!

Tiny Tailors

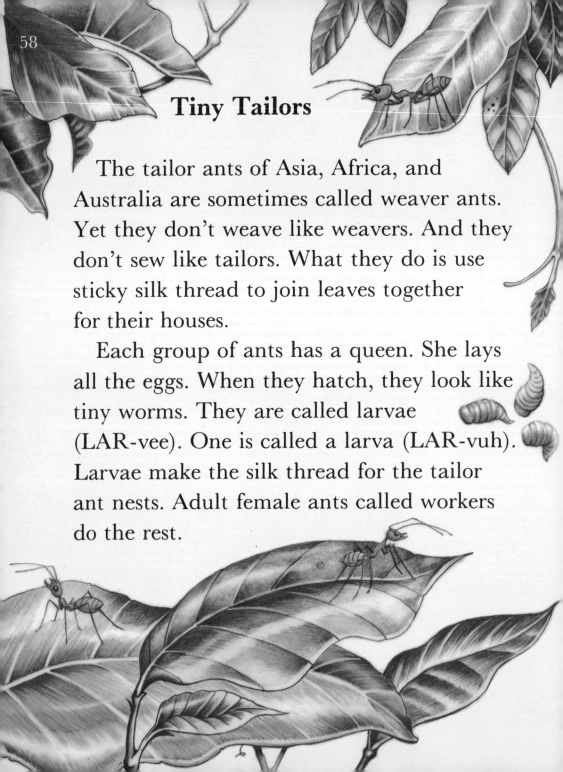

The tailor ants of Asia, Africa, and Australia are sometimes called weaver ants. Yet they don't weave like weavers. And they don't sew like tailors. What they do is use sticky silk thread to join leaves together for their houses.

Each group of ants has a queen. She lays all the eggs. When they hatch, they look like tiny worms. They are called larvae (LAR-vee). One is called a larva (LAR-vuh). Larvae make the silk thread for the tailor ant nests. Adult female ants called workers do the rest.

First a small group of workers pulls
two leaves together. Each ant grabs
the edge of one leaf with her jaws.
She holds on to the edge of a second
leaf with her feet. Then she pulls.
The leaves get closer together.

Sometimes there is a big
distance between leaves. One
ant can't reach all the way across.
So more workers help out. Groups of
tailor ants form chains. With her jaws,
each ant holds on to the waist of the ant
in front. The ants pull
together like a team in a
tug of war. They pull
until the leaves are close
together.

Now still more workers join them. Each worker carries a larva in her jaws. The worker ant squeezes the larva around the middle. It is something like squeezing a tube of toothpaste. But instead of toothpaste, a thread of silk comes out of the larva's mouth. The silk is a sticky liquid. It hardens when it touches the air.

Each worker ant moves her larva's head from one leaf to the other. Back and forth. Back and forth. Each time the silk thread touches a leaf, it sticks like glue. Lines of thread cross each other again and again. A strong silk web forms between the two leaves.

If the leaves are large, the ants need only two or three to start their nest. But more young are born all the time. The ants must make their nest bigger. They add leaf after leaf. Some nests get as big as a basketball! When the ants outgrow their nest, they build more nests.

Inside a nest are piles of eggs. Workers move in and out with larvae for nest building. Soldier ants guard the doors. But only the first nest has a queen.

No one seems to know much more about the insides of tailor ant nests. Why? Because the soldiers do such a good job. They bite anyone who comes too close!

Bubble Nests

Some fish make nests from bubbles. How strong can a bubble nest be? How long can a bubble nest last? You would be surprised!

Most fish have no real homes. They swim around in a large area. They let their eggs float in the water. Or they let them drop to the bottom. But a few fish build nests for their eggs and babies. The bubble nesters are among these.

Bubble nesters are sometimes called labyrinth (LAB-uh-rinth) fish. You can buy at least two kinds in a pet store. These are paradise fish and Siamese fighting fish. You can watch them make nests in their tanks.

First the male picks a spot for the nest.
Then he snaps at the air above the water.
He takes some air in his mouth and blows it
out under the water. It is a bubble! He
makes bubble after bubble after bubble.

The bubbles come together at the top of
the water. They pile up above the water,
too. They stick to a leaf or the side of the
tank. This is the bubble nest.

Why don't the bubbles break right away? In the male's mouth is a thick, sticky liquid called mucus (MEW-kuss). The mucus coats each bubble. It makes the bubbles strong.

At nesting time, the color of a male labyrinth fish gets brighter. He may be bright blue, red, or green. The color brings female labyrinth fish to him. Often one will come by while he is building the nest. But the male is not ready for her. Not yet. So he bites her! He chases her away.

Finally the nest is ready. Now any female that comes by is in luck. She does not get bitten. She lays her eggs in the water— up to 2,000 of them! At the same time the male fertilizes the eggs.

The eggs begin to sink. Both the male and the female chase after them. The fish catch the eggs in their mouths and spit them into the nest. The eggs stay between the bubbles. They are safe there.

Now the female's job is done. The male chases her away. But he stays with the nest. If any bubbles break, he makes new ones.

In two to four days, the eggs hatch. The father watches over the young fish. Any baby that swims away gets picked up in his mouth. Patooie! He spits it back into the nest.

Soon the babies are big enough to go out on their own. So the father swims away. The babies swim away. And the nest? It breaks up. The bubbles burst. Soon nothing of it is left at all.

A Nest for the Night

Would you like to sleep in a tree house every night? If so, you might like the life of a chimpanzee.

Chimps usually spend their days traveling. Small groups move around the African forest where they live. The chimps climb trees and eat fruit. They rest and clean each other's fur. Then they move on again. When evening comes, each chimp makes a nest to sleep in.

The chimps look for tall trees for their nests. High in the branches, they will be safe from snakes and hungry animals. Some of the chimps share a tree. Others choose their own trees nearby. Usually none of the trees has ripe fruit in it. So no animal will visit during the night to feed. No one will wake the chimps.

Each chimp finds one or two very big branches to build on. Sometimes the two branches form a V. The chimp stands on this base and grabs a nearby branch. He bends it over the base. He holds it down with his feet. Then he does the same with another branch. Then another and another. He uses both arms and both feet to build his nest.

The branches cross each other. They
weave in and out of each other under the
chimp's feet. The chimp bends down about
15 big branches in all. That is enough for a
good nest. He puts small branches and twigs
on top.

A mother chimp has a harder time
building her nest. She can use only one arm
and two feet. In the other arm she holds her
baby. The baby will sleep with her.

When the nest is ready, a chimp lies down in it. He wiggles around. He snaps off a few leafy twigs. He puts them under his head for a pillow. How comfortable! The chimp closes his eyes and goes to sleep.

The sun wakes the chimps early in the morning. Up they jump, and down they climb from their nests. They will probably never come back to them. That night the chimps will build new nests in other trees.

ABOUT THE AUTHOR AND ILLUSTRATOR

Hedda Nussbaum has liked animals ever since spending her childhood summers on a farm. She also likes plants, which she has written about in her earlier Step-Up Book, *Plants Do Amazing Things*, and in *Ranger Rick's Nature Magazine*. Besides being an author, Ms. Nussbaum is an editor of children's books. Previously she taught third and fourth grades and edited textbooks. She was born in New York City and lives there still. One of her favorite places in the city is the American Museum of Natural History.

Christopher Santoro became interested in art during high school in Bay Village, Ohio, where he drew cartoons for the school newspaper. He studied illustration at the Rhode Island School of Design and then moved to New York City. Before long he was busy illustrating books and doing advertising and design work. He has had drawings exhibited in the annual shows of the Society of Illustrators and the American Institute of Graphic Arts. When he isn't working, Mr. Santoro takes care of his two cats and gardens on his terrace.